IDEAS FOR
LEARNING ENVIRONMENTS

The articles presented in
this publication were
contributed by members
of the Austin Association
for the Education of
Young Children

naeyc

1834 Connecticut Avenue, N.W., Washington, D.C. 20009   (202) 232-8777

Photo Acknowledgments:

Jean Berlfein, Los Angeles, California, p. 53
Philip A. Biscuti, Connecticut College, New London,
   Connecticut, p. 55
Shirley I. Fisher, San Mateo, California, p. 50
Bruce Grossman, Corte Madera, California, p. 58
Steve Herzog, Modesto, California, p. 30
Michael D. Sullivan, Washington, D.C., p. 23

National Association for the Education of Young Children
1834 Connecticut Avenue, N.W., Washington, DC 20009

Library of Congress Catalog Card Number: 73-88182
ISBN Number: 0-912674-18-0
Printed in the United States of America. Second printing 1977.

Preface

    As members of the Austin Association for the Education of Young Children prepared and presented their monthly meetings in the late 1960s, they provided participants with many pages of invaluable ideas and experiences relating to the topic of each meeting. These pages were later compiled, expanded and refined to be sold as pamphlets at the Texas state meeting and local workshops. A favorable response to the pamphlets led to the addition of more topics, and the production of these publications became increasingly demanding. Volunteers were recruited to help with editing, typing, proofreading, printing and stapling. By the third year the collection included 20 pamphlets, and requests for them came from throughout the United States.

    In order to continue sharing these ideas with teachers on a broader scale, and as an expression of support of the national association, the Austin, Texas AEYC gave the collection of pamphlets to the National Association for the Education of Young Children for dissemination. Hopefully, this experience of the Austin AEYC, in meeting the needs of persons working with young children, will encourage other AEYC groups to move in their own positive directions.

Austin AEYC wishes to express its gratitude to the many hundreds of persons who have given of themselves and their talents in this effort, including:

Judy Avery
Jane Bauld
Betty Bennie
Ann Bone
Gayle M. Browne
Shirley Cannamore
Joni Cohan
Margaret A. Eppright
Priscilla P. Flawn
Linda S. Gwathmey
Janet Howard
Johanna Hulls
Ethel M. Kutac
Martha R. Loeffler
Sallie Beth Moore
Frances Morey
Mabel Pitts
Karen L. Quebe
Joan Sic Reine'
Jerry S. Turner
Polly H. Turner
Jeannette Watson
Mozella White
Jane M. Williams
Ouida Wright
University of Texas Child
  Development Laboratory
University of Texas at Austin
  Child Development
  Division
Schools and Centers of
  Austin

Contents

Planning — Focus on the Child

WHERE DO I BEGIN?

Planning begins with the child: Each child is unique and has his own way of responding to his world. In order for the teacher to plan effectively for the children in her group, she needs to know what each child is like, his level of development and his strengths and weaknesses.

Planning begins with teacher observation of the child in his play as he uses materials and interacts with other children. Throughout the day, the teacher observes for information which will help her understand the children she teaches. It is this knowledge about each child which provides the basic material for planning a curriculum that meets the individual growth needs of each child.

WHAT INFORMATION ABOUT EACH CHILD WILL BE HELPFUL TO THE TEACHER IN PLANNING?

The teacher will want to gather as much information about each child as possible. Specifically she will want to answer such questions as: What is the child like? What are his interests? What abilities, skills has he already developed? What is his home environment like? How does he respond to adults? How does he respond to other children? What motor skills has he developed? How does he express himself? What concepts or misconcepts has he developed? How does he solve problems? How does he approach materials? How does he learn best? What is he ready to learn?

As the teacher becomes more knowledgeable about each child, she is ready to plan specific objectives for him based on his level of development and special needs. A teacher's partial list of objectives might read:

John: To find a suitable outlet for hitting.

To develop skills for climbing.

To attend to an activity for more than two minutes.

Jim and Mary: To increase cutting skills.

To develop understanding of concepts such as "on," "under" and "above."

Jane: To help her to accept her new baby brother.

Kevin: To develop constructive means of sharing the tricycle with John.

To find constructive ways of entering into a group.

Mary, Kevin, Mark, Vickie:

To develop an understanding of "more" or "less."

To help them express themselves verbally.

Group:

To begin to develop the concepts of "large" and "small."

Using these and other objectives as a guide, the teacher begins to plan activities which provide learning opportunities for their attainment.

HOW DOES THE TEACHER DETERMINE WHAT ACTIVITIES AND MATERIALS SHE WILL PLAN

A teacher can use a variety of approaches for planning activities. One approach suggested by Nimnicht is *to look at the interest centers in the room and identify activities or materials which may be planned for each area.* Using this approach the teacher might plan the following activities to accomplish the objectives mentioned above:

John: *To find suitable outlets for hitting*
Art: Natural clay (Encourage John to squeeze, hit and pound.)
Manipulative toys: Pounding bench
Block area: Punching bag
Outdoors: Woodworking (with close supervision), boxing gloves

Jane: *To help accept new baby brother.*
Housekeeping Area: Dolls, baby bottles, clothing, doll bed and buggy
Books: Peter's Chair
Pictures: Pictures of families and babies in the room

Group· *To develop the concept of "large" and "small."*
Art: Place large and small sheets of paper in art area Have pasting projects with large and small pieces of scrap paper
Blocks: Provide contrast in size with blocks. Add

large and small trucks to block area.

Housekeeping Corner: Large and small cans, pots and pans, dolls

Manipulative: Nesting blocks, graduated shape puzzles, large and small beads with string

Books: The Little Fireman
        Pappa Small
        The Very Little Dog
        Clifford, The Big Red Dog
        The Biggest Bear
        Sizes

Music: Let's Make A Ball, Eency Weency Spider, Great Big Spider

Science: Collection of large and small rocks (Guide children to discuss differences in size as well as shapes and feel.)

Outdoor: Large cardboard box for children to play in, climbing structures of differing sizes, large and small cars in sandbox.

Choice of Activities: The teacher makes her choice of ACTIVITIES IN TERMS OF THE CHILDREN'S INTERESTS, THEIR LEVEL OF DEVELOPMENT, AND AVAILABLE MATERIALS AND RESOURCES. Another factor to consider is how children learn. Since children learn best through firsthand experiences, the teacher will want to provide many opportunities for the exploration of real items. It is important to have a variety of experiences available for children to touch, taste, smell and feel to use their senses in learning.

One teacher purchased a frozen fish from a fish market and placed it in a pan of water in the room. As the fish thawed, the children felt the fish's eyes, scales and fins and noted how it smelled. They wondered where it breathed and where it went to the bathroom. One child commented that the scales resembled her mother's contact lens. Another noticed that the dead fish could float in water but could not swim like the fish in the aquarium. This led to a discussion on the difference in things that are dead and things that are alive. Very few of these learnings would have occurred if the children had only seen a

4

picture of a fish or played with plastic or wooden ones.

Activities which involve the use of raw or unstructured materials are important to provide young children. Christianson in discussing the values of raw materials, states:

> So-called raw or unstructured materials are of special value in the play life of a child because they lend themselves to a wide gamut of possibilities for exploration and manipulation to creative activity; they stimulate imagination because of their lack of specific or representative form and satisfy children's needs in construction and dramatic play. Older children do not outgrow these materials but find new ways to use them in the realization of more complex purposes. Young children turn to art media and other manipulative materials interchangeably in accord with their needs and interest at the moment. [1]

Paints, clay, blocks and other unstructured materials should be available for children's use daily.

HOW WILL I PLAN FOR
THE DAY AND WEEK?

In planning for the day and week, the following suggestions will be of value.

> Plan for a broad range of activities in order to provide the children with many choices within their interests. This range should include activities from the following areas:

---

[1] Helen Christianson, Mary Rogers and Blanche Ludlum. *The Nursery School Adventure In Learning* (Boston: Houghton Mifflin Co., 1961) p. 86.

Art: Collage, cutting and pasting, clay, wood sculpturing, chalk, painting, crayons.

Dramatic Play: Housekeeping, doll-washing, nurse and doctor, different stores, baby play, cowboys, fireman, fishing, airplane play.

Science and Nature: Animals, insects, plants, rocks, shells and other collections, weather, seasonal changes.

Large and Small Motor Skills: Manipulative toys, climbing, structures, games involving motor skills.

Music: Songs, records, finger plays, creative movement, musical instruments.

Literature: Stories, poems, creative dramatization, filmstrips.

Concepts: Activities which foster development concepts of different size, shape and textures.

Outdoor Activities: Bubble blowing, clothes washing, climbing structures, art, dramatic play and other activities listed above.

Special and/or Small Group Activities: Cooking experiences, excursions, games, etc.

Don't move too fast in presenting new ideas or activities. Children need time to explore and experiment with materials and ideas thoroughly before expanding and elaborating on them. The younger the child, the more time is needed. Plan to repeat an activity throughout the year. With every exposure the child learns a new way of approaching the material and expands his concepts and understandings.

Sequencing activities for learning is important. The activities should be planned for the child to build basic concepts and later enlarge and expand upon them. For example, an orange may be placed on the science shelf for the children to touch, taste, feel, smell and observe different characteristics. The next day, oranges may be squeezed into orange juice as other properties are noted. Later, the orange may be compared with a grapefruit to identify likenesses and differences.

Consider the number of adults who will be available to supervise at a given time. If only one or two adults are present, avoid planning several activities in one time period which require close supervision (For example, finger painting, woodworking and water play).

In planning, flexibility is a must. As the teacher begins the day she follows the cues from the children and modifies her plans. At the end of each day she reviews her plans for the following day and revises them if necessary. She may decide to continue a successful activity or discontinue it if the children do not indicate interest. At other times additional activities suggested by the children's interests, conversation and play may be included.

PLANNING FOR EACH ACTIVITY

The success of any activity may be influenced by how it is presented and how prepared the teacher is for guiding the children in the activity. In planning for each activity the teacher will need to:

Identify possible learnings from the activity;

List materials which will be needed;

Determine how to set up the activity to stimulate the children to discover different possibilities for exploration;

Think through questions and comments the teacher can make to help children observe, see likenesses and differences, label and make generalizations. These comments should be at the child's level of thinking and understanding;

7

Try to anticipate questions which the children might ask in order to be better prepared to answer them. Many times children's ideas are of equal or greater value in learning than the ideas of the teacher. A well-prepared teacher can take advantage of the new learning avenues opened up by children.

Plan for ways to evaluate the activity and extend learnings through follow-up activities.

DAILY SCHEDULE

The daily schedule provides the basic structure for the day. When the schedule is planned for the group and is consistent from day to day, children feel secure and are free to explore their environment. Fewer discipline problems occur as children know what to expect, and less of the teacher and children's time is spent moving from one part of the day to another.

Since each group is unique, no one schedule is applicable for all groups of children or for all types of programs. Some children work best when they start the day outside, while others do better when the day begins inside. Some groups must have a scheduled time for rest while other groups need more flexible ways of incorporating times for rest in the day. When rooms and playyards are shared, the needs and tempo of other groups also are considered.

GUIDELINES FOR PLANNING THE SCHEDULE

Children are just learning to be members of a group. Since they are beginners, short blocks of time should be planned for large group activities such as music or story, while large blocks of time can be alloted for individual and small group activities.

Alternate times for active and quiet play. This helps children to pace themselves and prevents fatigue.

Plan routine times for toileting, handwashing, snacks and rest. In an all-day program, provision should be made for lunch and afternoon nap.

In planning routines, consider the age of the child. Two- and three-year-olds will need more scheduled times for toileting and rest. Four- and five-year-olds are more self-sufficient and require fewer scheduled times for toileting. With four- and five-year-olds, one may want to substitute a quiet activity in place of rest.

Since each group is different, the teacher may need to revise the schedule several times before arriving at one which is comfortable for her group. As the children change in interests and attention span during the year the schedule will again need revising.

Although the schedule for each group is different, the following format may serve as a guide.

SCHEDULE:

Half Day:

1-1½ hours	Indoor or outdoor self-selected activities.
30-40 minutes	Clean-up, toileting, snacks, music, story.
1-1½ hours	Outdoor or indoor self-selected activity.
15-30 minutes	Story and departure.

Order and time for activities may vary.

The activity planned at a particular time depends on what activity occurred in group time earlier in the day. One alteration is to have only one music or story time in the middle or at the end of the day.

All Day:

30-45 minutes	Breakfast (if served)
1-1½ hours	Indoor and outdoor self-selected activity.
30-40 minutes	Clean-up, toileting, snacks, music or story.
1-1½ hours	Indoor or outdoor self-selected activity.

30-40 minutes	Rest or quiet activity, story, toileting.
30-45 minutes	Lunch
15-30 minutes	Toileting
1½-2 hours	Nap (length will vary with age of group)
15 minutes	Snack (sometimes music and story are planned)
1-1½ hours	Indoor and outdoor self-selected activity (this may be divided into two time periods).
	Departure

WHAT DO I DO NEXT?

The planning process is a continuous cycle of looking at the child, identifying objectives, planning activities, guiding the activity in the classroom and evaluation. What does the teacher do after evaluation? She looks at the child again and identifies new interests, new levels of functioning and new objectives which serve as guides for planning new activities. This planning cycle occurs throughout each day, week and year as the teacher strives to create an environment which fosters learning and growth. If planning is focused on the child and his needs, the child is provided with many opportunities to develop into a healthy, well-adjusted individual capable of adapting to his world.

General Consideration

In this series of pamphlets the following two general areas are not discussed in detail. However, it is vitally important that special attention be given to concerns of children's health and safety as well as to promoting mutually positive, constructive parent-teacher relationships.

SOURCES FOR PLANNING

Baker, Katherine Read, Ed. *Ideas That Work with Children*. Washington, D. C.: NAEYC, 1972.

Dittman, Laura L. Ed. *Curriculum Is What Happens*. Washington, D. C.: NAEYC, 1970.

Leeper, S.H., Dales, R.J., Skipper, D.S. and Witherspoon, R.L. *Good Schools For Young Children*. New York: MacMillan Co., 1968.

Nimnicht, Glen, McAfee, Oralie, and Meies, John. *The New Nursery School Series*. New York: General Learning Corporation, 1969.

Todd, Vivian and Heffnam, Helen. *The Years Before School: Guiding Preschool Children*. New York: The MacMillian Co., 1969.

Creating Environments That Invite Learning

INTRODUCTION

Before planning for environments for young children (including physical facilities, equipment and materials), one must consider what the child is like, his nature and needs and how he learns. Most persons who have worked with young children note that the young child is active and vigorous and learns through concrete rather than abstract experiences. Therefore, physical facilities, equipment and materials provided for young children should be suitable for the development of children at their own maturity level and should be selected to allow for a wide range of abilities and patterns of growth.

The best learning environment (both indoor and outdoor) is one which stimulates the child to want to learn, to reach out for new understandings and new experiences, to inquire about his environment and to provide security. In order to create this type of learning environment, one must consider all physical facilities, equipment and materials carefully in their relationship to the total learning situation and select and use in accordance with the basic principles of child growth and development.

HEALTH AND SAFETY

The health and safety of preschool children are extremely important in any child care facility or school. A child's health affects his behavior, learning, feelings about himself, and his relationship with adults and other children. Therefore, each center should provide physical facilities which promote the health and safety of its children and should set up certain health policies and safety procedures and regulations.

INDOOR ENVIRONMENT

The indoor-learning environment should invite a child to participate in activities. Careful selection and arrangement of equipment and materials on the teacher's part help to provide such an environment. The teacher needs to be cautious as to the amount and variety of materials, as well as the timing for use of materials, so as not to overwhelm the child and at the same time provide enough to enable him to develop his potential. Also, she needs to consider the teacher-child ratio in her particular setting, for this will influence her room arrangement as well as tne number and kinds of activities she can provide at any given time. Some materials can be retained and drawn upon later when children are ready for new experiences.

The indoor environment needs to reflect the children's interests and activities. It should include equipment and materials that are: a) functional for the development of desired learnings; b) appropriate to age and maturity level; c) comfortable, friendly and warm from the child's point of view; d) always kept in good condition; and e) challenge the child to develop socially and emotionally as well as mentally and physically. It should provide a setting that promotes good health and is safe for all children.

Some recommendations for *locating and designing the indoor environment* include the following:

1. Provide a room that is large enough for children to live and work together cooperatively and freely. (Approximately 40-60 square feet per child is recommended).

2. Consider the shape and layout of the room. A rectangular-shaped room seems to lend itself more readily to activities than a square one and is more easily supervised than an L-shaped room.

3. Locate the room on the ground floor if possible and provide an entrance near the street level. Each room should be adjacent to toilet facilities.

4. Provide a room with satisfactory acoustics. Draperies, carpets on the floor, soft materials on walls and ceilings help to eliminate some sound as well as enhance beauty.

5. Select wall colors that will add to the light available in the room, such as yellow and other light colors. It is best if walls are washable at least to the height of children.

6. Provide wall space for both teacher- and-child-bulletin boards, remembering to locate the latter at the child's eye level.

7. Provide floors that are sanitary, easily cleaned, suited to hard wear, comfortable for children to set on and that deaden sound. Some suitable floor coverings include linoleum, a variety of woods, carpet, rubber or plastic tiles. A floor partly carpeted makes possible a comfortable arrangement for group time without the need for arranging chairs.

8. Provide sufficient number of windows low enough for children to see out, with some means of controlling light (shades, blinds).

9. Make sure the room has proper heat, light and ventilation.

10. Provide doors light in weight with low enough doorknobs so that children can handle them. It's best to have at least one door opening to the outside for safety reasons and easy access to playyard.

11. Provide a drinking fountain at child's level or some means for children to get a drink of water independently.

12. Make some provision for rest and relaxation periods. (This would be essential in a full-day program.) Cots, pads, mats, small rugs or blankets are frequently used for the rest period. Space should also be provided to store these.

13. Running water and sinks are essential for preparing and cleaning up after school activities. The toilet and handwashing facilities should be adjacent to or easily accessible to both indoor and outdoor areas. Provide at least one lavatory and one toilet for every ten children,

making sure they are of suitable size or height for the child's accessibility and independence in use (toilet seat 10-13 inches from floor or ramp and lavatories 23-24 inches from floor or ramp).

14. Provide storage space for equipment in daily use by children at their own level so they can learn responsibility in putting things away. Also provide at least one large storage cabinet in the room for the teacher to keep things out of reach of the children. It is preferable to have other storage areas in another room for toys and materials not in use.

Choosing Flexible Equipment and Furnishings

Adaptability is a highly valued characteristic of a pre-school setting. Young children's needs require that the site and the space, along with the furniture and equipment, permit rapid changes. Some items that facilitate this are: screens, portable cabinets, bookcases, tables or carts. Any classroom can be used in a flexible way through the arrangement of furnishings.

Besides being portable, furniture should be durable, comfortable, attractive, child-sized, storable and easily cleaned. Some of the basic portable furnishings would include chairs, tables, shelves and lockers.

Chairs: should be stackable for storage, light enough for children to handle, movable without undue noise and the proper height for children (approximately 15-20 inches high depending on age and size of children). Since chairs are frequently used at tables, it is best that they not have arms. Other types of seating arrangements add variety to your environment such as rocking chairs, benches, stools or even floor mats in the home center or library area.

Tables: should be varied to meet needs of children and activities. Proper height is from 15 to 22 inches. In most groups you will have children of varying sizes, so you will need at least two heights of tables and chairs. Contour stack tables are recommended for easy storage and rubber tips on legs lessen noise. Tables accommodating from four to six children are generally advisable for preschoolers. Table shape may vary according to needs and space available. Rectangular tables are better for some art activities involving large sheets of paper. Small tables designed to be used singly or in combinations are quite versatile. It's desirable to have some tables with washable surfaces such as formica.

Shelves: should be low; open shelves and display units give children a chance to see, touch, think about, ask questions and choose materials independently. Doors on shelves take up valuable floor space and are a possible hazard. Where shelves have to be closed, sliding doors are preferred. Shelves that are sturdy, but easy to move, are more flexible in room arrangement and create centers of interest. Bulletin board or pegboard backing helps convert the unit for dual use.

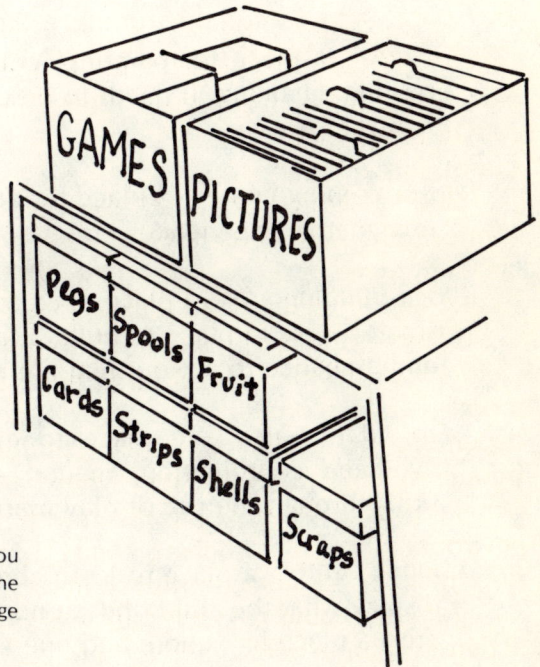

Here's an example of how you can organize and make the best use of available storage space of teacher materials.

Lockers: Planning for children's personal belongings is important. It is a way of showing respect for children and providing opportunities for their independence. Lockers should be low enough for children to reach, near the child's play area and labeled distinctively with pictures, names, colors, etc. You can have lockers built or purchased or make your own with boxes or ice cream cartons. Movable lockers can serve as room-dividers if they do not tip over easily. (Other small equipment will be discussed in the pamphlet on indoor equipment.) Movable storage cabinets are preferable to many built-ins, which may prevent flexible use of wall space.

Centers of Interest

In most programs, space arrangements are designed around common activities in interest centers. These centers would usually include:

Art area - a place for painting, collage-making, cutting, pasting, chalking. It needs to be placed near water and light.

Housekeeping center - a place for acting out familiar and imaginative experiences.

Block-building area - a place to create with both large and small blocks, a place to build a farm, a boat, airplane, and a chance to act out real-life roles.

Manipulative area - a place to enhance motor skills, eye-hand coordination, mental, language and social skills through the use of play materials.

Science center - a place to learn about nature; a place to display what the child finds at home, on a nature walk, etc.; a place to explore and question.

Music center - a place for listening to records, singing, creating dance and playing musical instruments.

Book and quiet area - a place to be alone, quiet in one's thoughts; a place to explore the world in books.

The following sample-room arrangement displays how these areas can be designed and considers some of the other functional aspects in organization of space reviewed in this pamphlet.

Some Suggestions for Room Arrangement

You will want to arrange your room and organize equipment so:

Your children will feel comfortable and secure. Before new children arrive, arrange your room carefully. Keep it that way, if possible, until the children are accustomed to the arrangement and sure of themselves.

If you have to convert your room for lunch or nap, do this the same way every day. Minimize confusion by moving into the change gradually.

The children will become increasingly independent.. Start teaching them from the beginning where everything they use is kept. When you change toys, put the same type in the same place.

Refer to your interest areas and equipment by name, for instance, "science center" or "wastebasket." Then you can say to a child, "Have you looked in the science center to see if our beans are sprouting?" He will go independently to examine the beans.

Later you will need to make changes to introduce new

ROOM PLAN

Room size 536 square feet

Maximum capacity 15 children

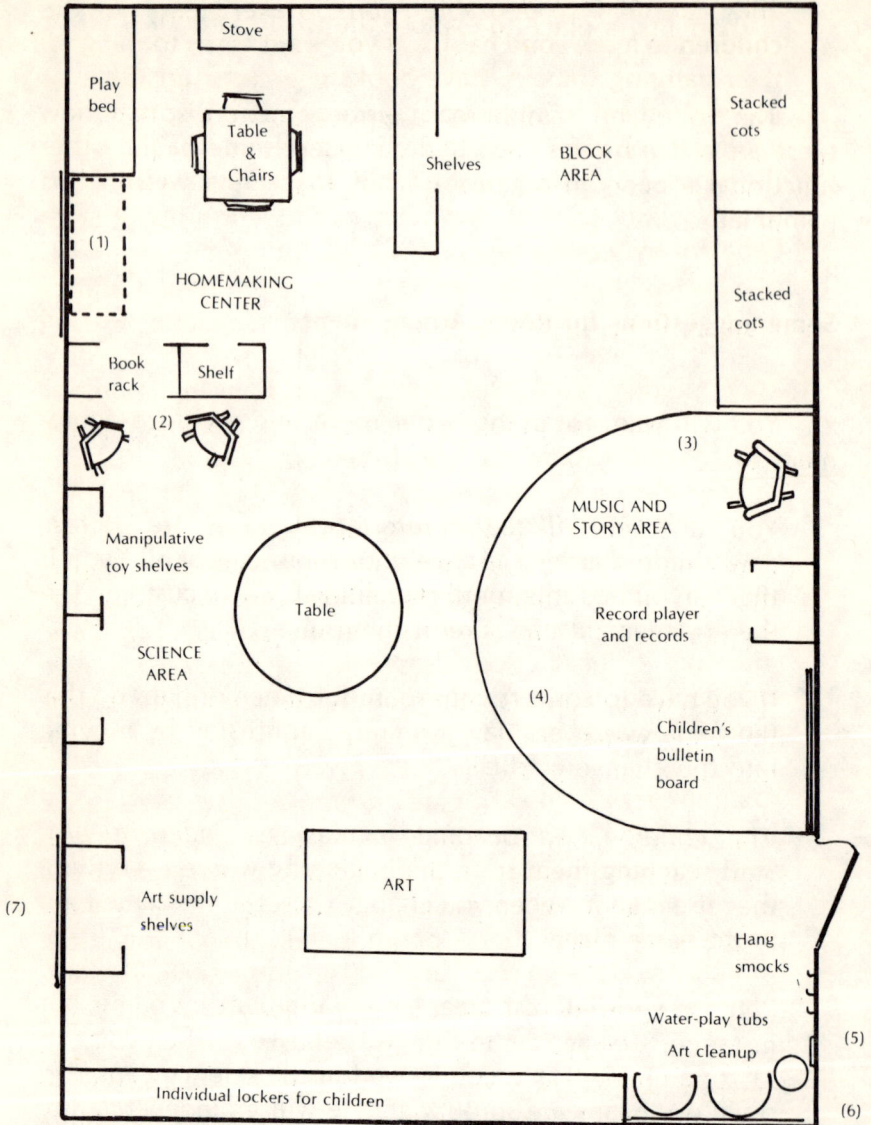

Stove

Play bed

Table & Chairs

(1)

HOMEMAKING CENTER

Shelves

BLOCK AREA

Stacked cots

Stacked cots

Book rack

Shelf

(2)

Manipulative toy shelves

(3)

MUSIC AND STORY AREA

Record player and records

Table

SCIENCE AREA

(4)

Children's bulletin board

ART

Art supply shelves

(7)

Hang smocks

Water-play tubs

Art cleanup

(5)

Individual lockers for children

(6)

1 A second bed or folding mat
2 Child-size rocking chairs
3 Adult rocking chair

4 Rug
5 Wastebasket and paper towels
6 Adult bulletin board above tubs

7 Windows

20

experiences and stimulate interest. By then the children can find what they want without wandering around.

They can develop desirable habits. Make it easy for the children to learn good habits. If you want them to hang up their painting smocks, have hooks near your art table. If you want them to clean up spills, have cleaning materials handy. If you want them to work puzzles on a table, place the puzzles on a shelf near a table. If you don't want them to run wildly up and down the room, don't invite such behavior by leaving long, open areas of floor space. And, of course, children are much more likely to put things away if they understand where the things belong.

Your children can work together with a minimum of friction. Be sure your interest areas are located in different sections of the room and are all interesting so the children will not always be congregating in one spot. Set up areas with such clarity that they are suggestive of the activity therein. For example, a record player and musical instruments designate music activity. Also allow some means for expansion or contraction of certain areas. For your immature children, provide several of the same items, such as little trucks by the blocks or three irons in the homemaking center.

Your children can have privacy if they desire it. (We know they need it.) Try to provide privacy for the individual child through the location of your book area, listening-to-records area, science center or their own locker. Many times creative work, block-building, etc., need protection from traffic. Arrange your room so the noisier activities are away from the quieter ones.

References:
Leeper, Dales, Skipper, Witherspoon, *Good Schools for Young Children.* New York: The MacMillan Co., 1971.
Texas Day Care, State Department of Public Welfare, Austin, Texas.

You can have a story group or active music without much shuffling of equipment.

You, the teacher, are released for teaching. You shouldn't have to run yourself ragged telling children where things are, getting things out or constantly nagging at children to do things.

Whether your room is tiny or large, is shared with another group or is a partitioned section of an auditorium, it can still be a self-contained teaching unit which belongs to your group of children. You, the teacher, are the most important factor in creating an effective and creative environment for learning.

LEARNING IN THE PLAYYARD

Your yard is your second classroom and is as important as the indoors. We all know that playing outdoors is necessary for physical development. Let's think of it also as a place for intellectual and social growth.

When we initially prepare our indoor room for teaching, we consider many things: big basic equipment, the arrangement of centers, teaching materials, etc. We plan daily for a variety of interesting, challenging experiences. Why not look at the outdoors with the same perspective?

The Basic Yard: First, meet the requirements of square footage per child. For safety and convenience, plan to enter the yard directly from the school. Also, for safety, see that there are no blind spots. That is why square, rectangular or *L-* shaped yards are superior to *T-* or *U*-shaped ones. Many schools solve the problem by dividing the latter shapes into two yards, connected by double gates. Only one yard is used when a single teacher is outside. This also permits the highly recommended plan of keeping small groups intact and always with their own teacher. (Several groups together, even though space is adequate, are not desirable.)

Once in a while, a fortunate few find themselves with the ideal yard. Most of us have to plan long-range and work to get it.

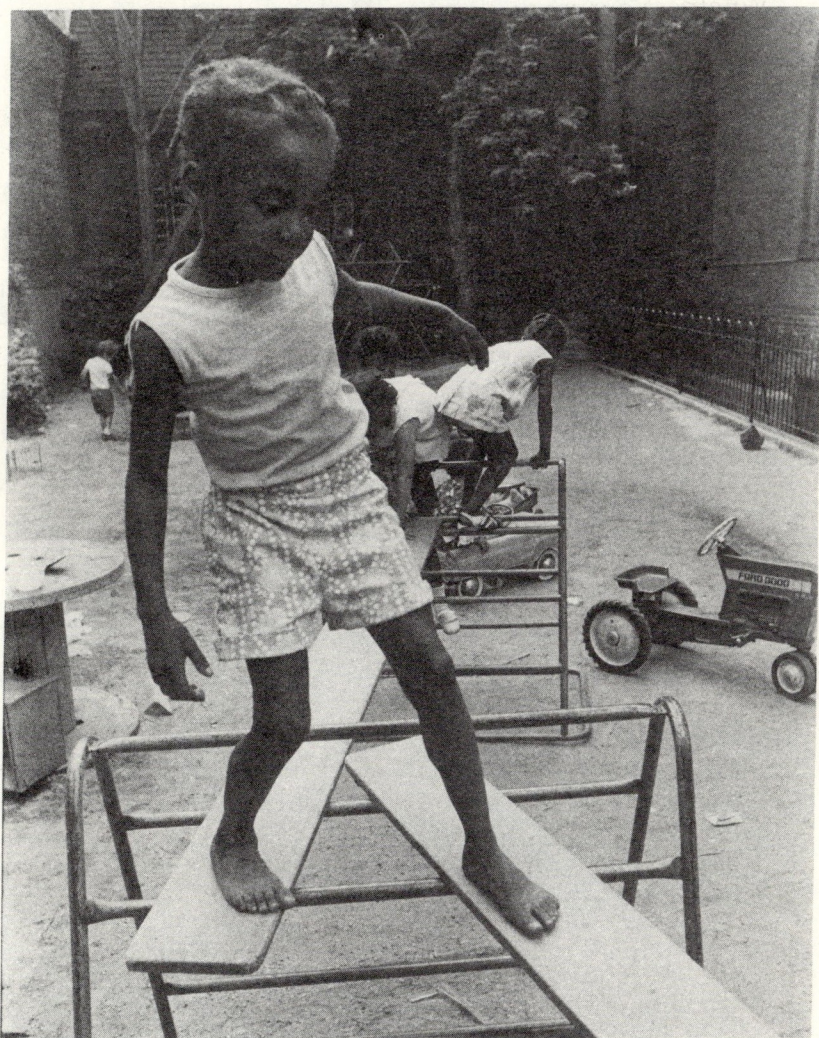

Surface: Plan for several surfaces. This in itself provides a variety of experiences for the children. Conventionally we think of a flat, smooth yard as best. This is not true. Leave part of your yard uneven or deliberately make it uneven with a pile of dirt or a section of sewer pipe covered with dirt. Work toward having:

A *grassy area:* Sod with a grass resistant to traffic and dry weather. Bermuda grass can be grown satisfactorily from seed but it requires about six weeks or so to become established before it can bear traffic.

A *hard-surfaced area/or walks:* (preferably circular) where wheel-toys roll easily. (Hard-packed dirt works for this fairly well but it obviously cannot be used immediately after rains.)

A *section with rich soil:* where the children can cultivate their own vegetables and flowers. This is usually more satisfactory if it is long and narrow, away from traffic and close to the building or fence.

A *digging area* plus a sandbox.

A *small rock or gravel area.*

Fence: Consider a strong chain-link fence as providing more than protection and privacy:

Plant vines (such as honeysuckle, gourd, morning glories) by the fence or fasten plastic bottles or other unbreakable containers filled with growing plants to the fence.

Attach a homemade weathervane, anomometer and water gauge for experiences with weather.

Tie a length of hose for pretend filling stations, telephones, etc., to the fence.

24

Use the fence for bird feeders and birdbaths until your trees grow.

Drinking Fountain: Children can much more readily get the water they need if a fountain is accessible outdoors.

Trees and shrubs: Choose safe and hardy trees and shrubs which are particularly adaptable to your region. Trees are needed for shade. Trees and shrubs are needed for beauty and for year-around nature experiences. (Many feel children benefit as much by walking down the street to see a flowering shrubs. They do not. They must literally live with every stage of growth to reap maximum benefits.)

Once you have a variety of plant life, you should have birds and insects too. You may be fortunate enough to attract lizards, horned toads, frogs and turtles.

Trees should not be planted where, at maturity, they are likely to endanger the safety of the building or exclude light or air from rooms. They should be safe, not likely to lose heavy branches nor be struck by lightening. Some of the faster growing trees are not desirable because they are susceptible to disease and pests. They also have soft brittle wood and weak crotches which make climbing dangerous.

When planting trees, consider what the shade is needed for and at what time of the day. Remember that a heavy, dense tree will produce deep shade; an open tree will filter light. Trees near the street must be of medium size with deep root systems. Consider the location of telephone and power lines, the location of large equipment, the location of other trees. Trees need enough open ground around them to obtain food elements and water.

Take care to select nonpoisonous shrubs for the playyard. Consult local nurserymen about safe varieties in a specific region.

Animals: Provide a large outdoor cage for visiting animals and fowls or those belonging to the center. (Be sure to check city health regulations before you actually get the animals.) Also, have the animal's health checked and plan for continued care. The suitability of a particular animal or bird for a group of young children should be investigated.

Sandbox: Plan for a sandbox or several tractor tires placed together or some means for the children to have a place for playing in sand and dirt. This is a *must!* A sandbox requires no bottom but it *should* be large enough for several children - possibly fifteen feet long and five feet wide or an odd shape.

Provide sugar scoops, sturdy, safe kitchen utensils, plastic bottles made into pails, bowls, funnels, cups, sprinklers, etc. Steam shovels, tractors and trucks are good, too.

Play Equipment

A jungle gym, a slide and swings are fine (unless they are too big to be used safely with small children and then they should be cut off or the stands put deeper in the ground). Check to see that all three are in placement out of traffic areas. Swings with rubber seats also provide for additional safety. For your yard to become a learning situation, smaller movable equipment to encourage creative play must be provided:

boards with cleats for balancing, sliding and jumping
ladders 6' long
sawhorses (12" and 18" high)
ladder box
tunnel barrels on stands (removable)
sturdy wooden boxes of assorted sizes (42"x30"x30", 35"x23"x16" and smaller)
hollow blocks (51/2"x11"x11", 51/2"x11"x22")
rocking boat
climbing sawhorse

Look around for inexpensive or discarded objects, such as:

cable spools	sewer pipes
tires and inner tubes	railroad ties
utility poles	tree trunk
kegs	packing boxes
display racks (as for carpets)	tables cut off (durable enough to climb on)

Wheel Toys

Purchase durable tricycles, wagons, wheelbarrows. When budgets are limited, it is suggested that more than one tricycle should be purchased rather than a variety of different kinds of wheel toys. Make carts, flatcars, wheelbarrows and sleds. Use discarded wheels or ballbearing casters. Loops of rope threaded through a piece of hose make good handles.

Outdoor Storage

Every school needs outdoor storage space! If there is nothing available such as under-the-house storage room, plan for a unit that will serve the dual purpose of a playhouse, climbing device, etc., and storage. Make it low or place it so the teacher will not have a supervision problem.

Wheel toys particularly occupy valuable space inside on bad days and the children miss the opportunity of choosing equipment from the storage unit and then putting it away.

Planning Your Yard

Draw a scale model of your yard and plan where everything should go. Otherwise, you may find you have planted a tree where the jungle gym belongs or that the children have no place for a garden.

Here are a few things to remember when planning:

* Place your jungle gym in an open area (perhaps the grassy section) so the children can use their small, moveable equipment like the boards with it.

27

* The swing should be placed where the children will not be running, riding behind or close in front of it.

* Point the slide so that children will not slide down in the path of traveling wheel toys.

* Place storage units close to a hard-surfaced area or connect them with a walk.

* Plan the garden away from traffic and away from shrubs and trees, but near a water outlet if possible.

* The sandbox and digging area need to be out of the line of traffic and shaded (except in the winter, so do not use an evergreen for shade).

* Unless money is available for many trees, plant them where the children will benefit by their shade all day.

* Consider how the yard looks to parents, casual observers, etc. Plant some of the shrubs so they can enjoy them, too. If the yard is away from the entrance, make the entrance attractive with growing things.

Notes just for the teachers

You may need to do a little more physical labor as your yard develops, but having busy, happy children is truly rewarding.

The workload can be minimized if all the teachers assume specific responsibilities and take turns:

getting things out;
making new arrangements to keep the yard challenging to children;
watering trees, shrubs, grass, flowers;
sprinkling yard sections that are dusty;

* Perforated hardboard, or pegboard, lends to displays. Golf tees fit into the pegboard holes to make useful hanging devices.

* Plywood is classified by thickness and number of plies. If the edges are to be left exposed, fill in the cavities along the edge with a kind of plaster called "spackle" before painting.

* Particle board does not tend to warp and can be covered easily with one coat of paint. This board cannot hold screws against strong tension.

* Foam plastic is porous core faced on two sides with paper. This is excellent when weight is a consideration, but it is not widely available.

* Celotex wall and ceiling board is available in large sizes. It easily takes thumbtacks, but holes remain.

* Cork sheets or pressed cork chips are available in natural colors and in various thicknesses.

* Fabric scroll Sew a hem at one end of a length of fabric wide enough to insert a dowel (1-inch in diameter will give you the weight and rigidity you need). After sliding in the dowel and stapling from the back through the fabric, insert a screweye in each end of the dowel and tie a cord or nylon filament fishline from one eye to the other. Measure the length of scroll you want and make hem for dowel at the bottom also.

---

* *Display and Exhibit Handbook,* Wm. Hayett. New York: Reinhold Publishers, 1967.

- Affixing the Bulletin Board

  * Wire and screweyes - If the bulletin board is framed, these are used by attaching to the back of the frame.
  * Adhesive-backed fabric patch can be used for lightweight boards.
  * Double-backed cellophane tape is used for lightweight boards.

  * Double-backed sponge tape - sponge core allows for more weight of board.
  * Stringing: Pierce holes near two top corners and loop strong thread or thin string for hanging.
  * Easels   are made by attaching a cardboard support to the back of a lightweight board. This can be made simply by folding cardboard to form a right angle and gluing it to the back of the bulletin board. Trim at the bottom so that the bulletin board slants backward.

- Backdrops

  * Paper (poster paper, silk-screened paper, construction or flint paper)
  * Cork
  * Paint (laquer spray, roller painting, brush painting)
  * Fabric (felt, burlap, flannel, denim, muslin)
  * Shelfpaper
  * Blotters
  * Wallpaper

Mount papers onto bulletin board on backside with stapler. In some instances, as with fabric onto cardboard, rubber cement can be used. Do not attempt pleated or draped effects with fabric.

• Lettering

Commercial

* *Plaster ceramic letters* are available in many different styles, sizes and depths with smooth backs for gluing, with pin backs for pressing into a suitable surface or with a broad base for free standing.

* *Spine letters* are letters cast together on a center spine from which individual letters can be broken for use. Backs are plain or pressure sensitive.

* *Pressure-sensitive letters,* available in vinyl or paper, can be removed from their backing sheet and pressed firmly on the bulletin board. Vinyl letters do not tear or deteriorate; the paper letters are very inexpensive.

* *Embossing machines* which print raised letters on a plastic self-adhesive tape are available for printing on a variety of colors and in various widths.

* *Stencil precut letters* are available in every size and style. Letters are formed by tracing the outline or by filling the pattern with ink.

* *Alphabet templates* are usually rigid thin clear plastic for tracing without smearing ink.

* *Typewriting* on good quality paper will solve the problem of an extended text needed for communicating an idea. It will be necessary for people to be able to come close for reading.

* *Felt-tip* markers are available for freehand lettering, for highlighting with color and for underlining. Colors and widths vary greatly.

* *Broad-point pens* used with an opaque ink requires practice to get a smooth application.

Homemade

* Letters and numbers can be drawn on cardboard and cut out carefully with an exacto knife. Save the cutout forms as well as the board to be reused.

* Letters can be cut from corrugated cardboard, "core-buff" (only one side of the corrugated cardboard fluting

is faced), textiles, carpets, cork sheets, blotters, textured paper.

* Roving, rope, string, yarn, cord (including electric cords), raffia, wire or leather strips can be formed and pinned to make words or phrases.
* Map pins with colored beads are decorative and three-dimensional when placed side by side to form letters and words.

• Mounting Materials

* Rubber cement: practical for mounting photographs, drawings, lettering because it is easy to apply and can be permanent or nonpermanent. To be permanent, apply rubber cement to both surfaces to be bonded and allow to dry before mounting. To be nonpermanent, mount before rubber cement has dried or dissolve the cement bond with rubber cement thinner.

* Permanent bonding: milky white glue compounds which dry clear will permanently bond all porous materials.

* Dry-mounting pictures: with electric iron on "low," touch piece of dry-mounting tissue onto back of picture; trim picture and tissue together. Place on mounting material and touch corners of picture with electric iron (on "low"), then cover with butcher paper and iron from the center to edges with slow steady strokes.

* Double-backed cellophane tape: used for nonpermanent, lightweight mounting.

* Push pins:	come in colored heads, glass and aluminum beads and in several lengths.
* Map pins:	colored beads are decorative and practical.
* Staple gun:	simplest and fastest method of mounting.
* Peg board fittings:	can be mounted on cardboard if awl or nail holes are made for the fittings. Make sure the holes are spaced carefully and straight.

CHILDREN'S BULLETIN BOARDS

• How to use a bulletin board for children

    * Place at *eye-level* for children.
    * Change often.
    * Vary techniques and textures.

    Example: A picture of a cowboy on a horse could be mounted on a plain textured construction paper with narrow border and then placed upon textured wallpaper of western print.

    Example: A picture of children in lacy dress-up scarves could be mounted on complementing paper and a ruffled lace strip could be glued around the outside edge of the paper.

    Example: A farm picture could be mounted on a natural straw mat.

    * Place strategically in the room a few select pictures; but your bulletin board should hold a little extra surprise, something *real* to encourage questions or further exploration.

Example: A mounted picture of a turkey surrounded by turkey feathers.

Example: A mounted picture of fish in an aquarium with a draped fishnet under the corner of the mounting.

Example: A mounted picture of a policeman surrounded by bright traffic signs.

* Mount black and white prints on any color mounting board. Smaller pictures can be grouped together. When mounting color pictures, use complementing color backgrounds. With pictures of similar subjects, use the same background color.

* Give children the opportunity to *help create* the bulletin board. Not only does this increase their awareness of the presence of the bulletin board, but it is an excellent means for creative expression, exploration, questioning, clarifying concepts.

Example: For an art experience, allow children to create the sea and land on large brown butcher paper. Paint applied by a wad of newspaper gives an interesting mottled effect. Pictures of things found in the sea - deep-sea divers, boats, shells, fish - and things of the land are made available for placement by the children.

Example: Families is another subject which can be effectively presented. Cutouts of various family members (with flannel applied to the back, will cling to flannel, burlap or other coarse fabric) can be manipulated by children with much creative expression.

• Why use pictures?

* To enlarge and enrich experiences.
* To help develop appreciation of good art.

* To add to knowledge.
* To help children accept ideas.
* To add to a pleasing environment.

• How to select pictures for young children

  * Pictures should be large and realistic.
  * Bright primary colors are best.
  * Have one center of interest.
  * Subject matter should be appropriate for the maturation level of the children.
  * Emphasize a theme.

• Where to find good pictures

Magazines	Newspapers
Calendars	Catalogs
Book jackets	Children's original creations
Grocery store displays	Record covers
Photographs	Commercial picture stories
Wrapping paper	Greeting cards
Wall paper	Picture postcards
	Books beyond repair

PARENT BULLETIN BOARDS

Well-planned bulletin boards are an important means of communication between teachers and parents and help to give the school a pleasant atmosphere.

• Facts to remember:

  * People read left to right and not much above eye level.
  * The most effective bulletin board contains a single idea which is recognizable at a glance.

* Cost and teacher time are to be kept to a minimum.
* The entire presentation should be completed before leaving it!

- Topics for Parent Bulletin Boards

The following list of captions and ideas is given only to begin your creative thinking. Every parent group is unique, every teacher is unique in her own experiences; therefore, consider your own group in creating topics.

"Cook Up Fun" - kitchen experience at home.
"Fun for Small Travelers" -activities during vehicle travel.
"Book Power" - old favorites or new books.
"Cost-Nothing Fun" - art materials at home.
"Nature through a Child's Eye" - science experiences.
"Interested in Car Pooling?" - a city map with map pins marking children's addresses help parents work out car pools.
"Mom, Dad and Me" - family relations (this can be varied according to family members represented in your group).
"Self-Help--How to Encourage It" - garments which encourage independence.
"Friendship is Like a Tree which Grows and Grows" children enjoying being together.
"To a Friend's House, the Road is Never Long" - good topic before summer vacation encouraging visiting during holidays.
"The Life You Save May Be Your Child's" - home dangers.
"A Well-Rounded Program" - parts of the school's program presented between wheel spokes.

"Must a Child Share?" -present a question without giving an answer to direct parents to helpful pamphlets.

"What Does Nursery School Teach" -photos of nursery school learning experiences.

"Kindergarten Learnings from A to Z" - learning experiences from agriculture to zoology (with each letter of the alphabet representing another experience). This could be a series over a period of time.

"Current Events Day" -clippings from newspapers, news magazines, notices of community events (i.e., lectures, children art shows, workshops or symposiums sponsored by professional groups), and recent legislative action in areas of education.

"Our Staff...on the Know"- information about teacher education or enrichment before state conventions or other events that affect teaching staff.

RESOURCE READING FOR PARENT BULLETIN BOARDS

Dent, *Bulletin Boards for Teaching*

Lane and Tolleris, *Planning Your Exhibit*

Moore and Richards, *Teaching in the Nursery School*

Homemade and Improvised Equipment

Equipment must contribute to the development of a young child. A child responds and reacts to equipment provided for him. The first consideration when planning, buying or building equipment is the young child. Unless equipment is selected with knowledge of how a child learns, it may become an expensive and needless addition to the center. How do children learn in their early years? They learn through direct experience, their senses, manipulation and active experimentation of their environment and the responses of other people.

An excellent advantage of equipment illustrated in this booklet is that it can be made by most teachers and volunteers. Involvement of staff and parents does more than build equipment; it builds a cooperative and understanding spirit helpful to all. Equipment should involve the child; the making of equipment should involve the teacher and parents.

Teacher- or volunteer-made equipment offers an economical approach to the providing of equipment for young children. Homemade equipment can supplement commercial products or be the basis of your equipment inventory. The illustrations in this booklet are economical, easy to build, safe

42

and durable when properly constructed. Donated building materials can lower the cost even more. Before purchasing raw materials you should consider the following:

Is the project what the center needs and what you want?

Will you or the volunteers have time to complete the project after you start?
Will you have to buy more materials than you really need? Will the total material cost including the surplus represent a savings over commercial equipment?

Do you have the necessary tools? All the equipment in this book can be built with common hand tools.

Are there volunteers available to help you? Could you delegate the project to a volunteer?

A child must have equipment to learn. This book offers some easy and economical methods to provide that equipment. Good luck and happy building.

OUTDOOR EQUIPMENT

SAWHORSE

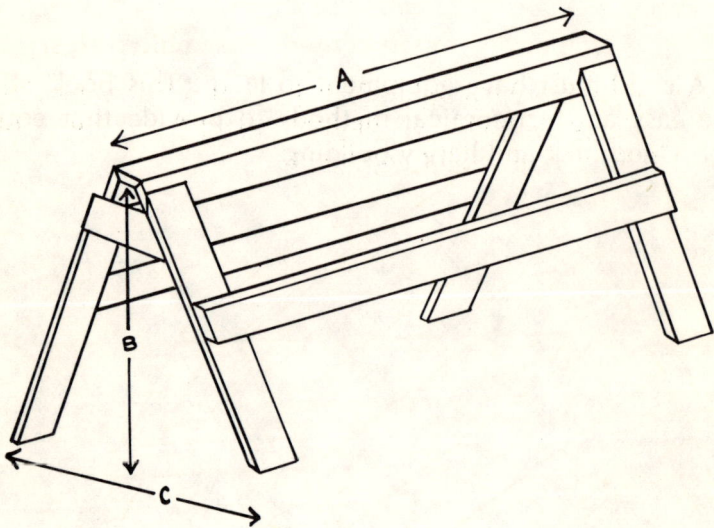

A -- 21" or 22"
B -- 12" or 18"
C -- 10" or 12"

CLIMBING HORSE

Excellent for large-muscle development. Children enjoy social and dramatic play on and under this.

Variations: 1. Construct 8-foot boards with cleats. Use on cross-pieces at different heights for climbing
2. Construct smaller sawhorses, using comparable plan.
3. Use inside or out.
4. Cover occasionally with an old bedspread for a tent.
5. Turn on end and place next to the wall for a pretend cage.

Note: Plane edges, round corners. Assemble with screws.

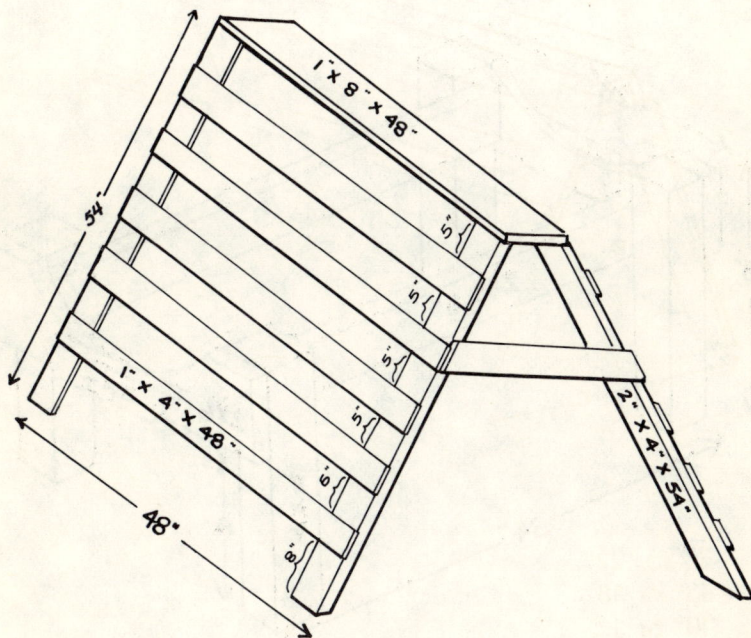

BARREL STAND

Designed to support metal or wooden barrels (with open ends). Excellent for imaginative play.

Addition of slats between the 2" x 6" cross-pieces (underneath) provides another challenging piece of equipment.

Length depends on barrel height. Plan for approximately 32".

Arc depends on barrel radius. Approximately 21" across, 6" deep.

Safety measure to prevent barrel slipping off.

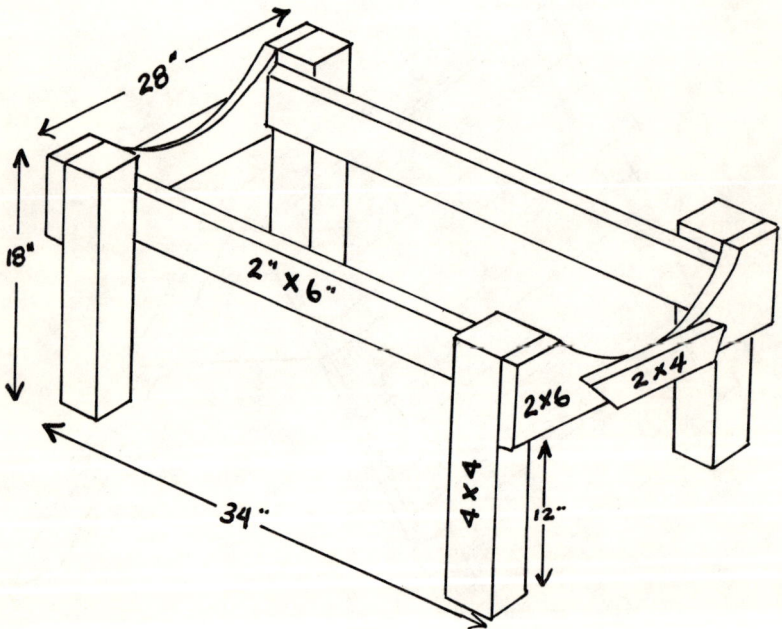

SLAT BOX

This provides opportunity for social and imaginative play as well as for physical exercise.

Variations:

1. Construct a second slat box with the top solid.
2. Construct 48" x 48" x 48".
3. Construct two 50" boards with cleats so these fit snugly inside box between side slats.

Note: Space between slats must be at least 8" so children can crawl through. Bottom is open. Assemble with screws. Plane edges, round corners, sand and paint.

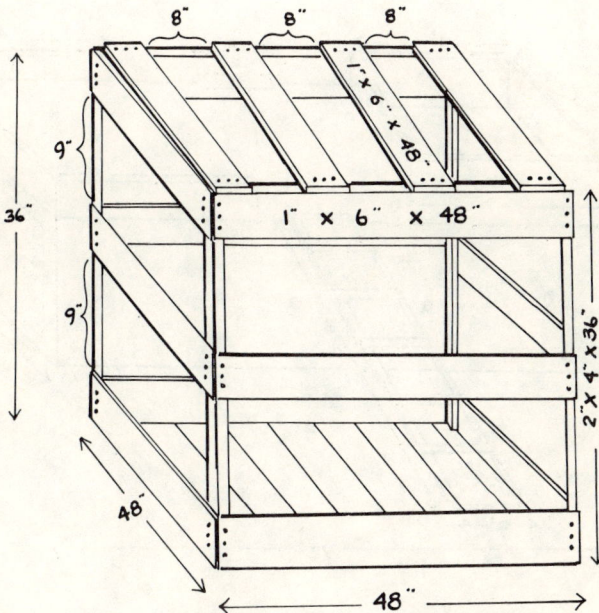

COMBINATION OUTDOOR STORAGE SHED, PLAYHOUSE AND EQUIPMENT DESIGNED FOR IMAGINATIVE PLAY

A. Make doors on both ends as large as possible so tricycles and wagons can be rolled in easily.

B. Fasten box to top for imaginative play (or make frame and secure it), 3' wide, 4' long, 12" deep.

C. Construct railing along edge for interest and for social play, 4' long, 1' high.

D. Attach 8' x 10" x 1" board (smooth) on the other side.

E. Attach 6' x 10" x 1" board with cleats space 12" apart on one side.

Note: To prevent wheel toys from being stolen, it is recommended that the bottom be solid. Round corners.

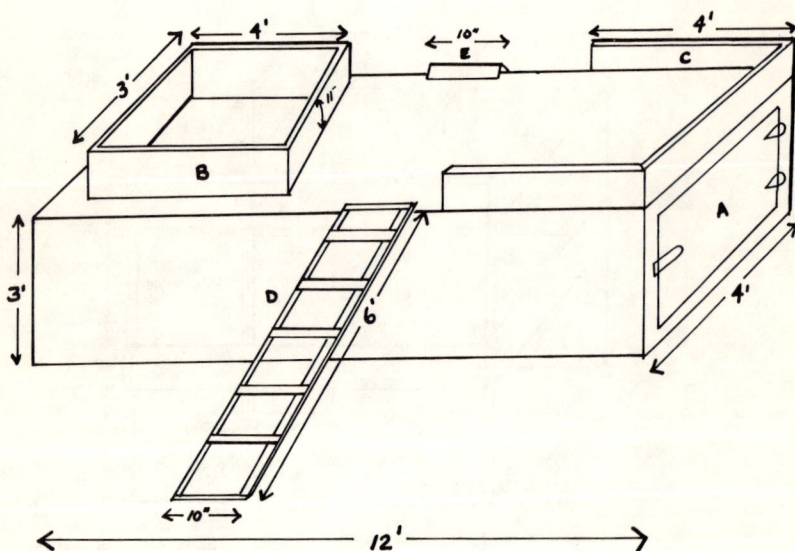

BOARDS WITH CLEATS

A must for physical development and imaginative play!
Use for ramp, balancing board, bouncing board, etc.
Plan at least four for a yard.
   Size: Boards: 1″ x 10″ x 8′
         Cleats: 1″ x 10″ x 2″
Fasten with screws, 2″ from end.

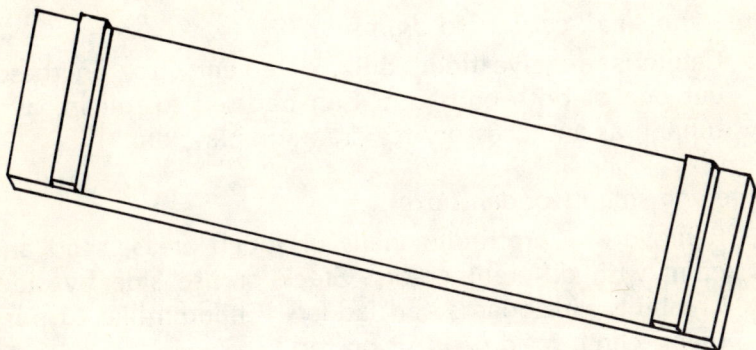

Do Your Own Thing
Improvised Outdoor Equipment

Slides.....

   They can be made out of sawhorses, boards with cleats
and boxes.

Cable Spools.....

   Obtain large spools from the telephone company (they are
used to roll wire on). Remove any rough parts and sand

smooth. Paint the spools and use as tables and chairs. Children like to roll, climb, jump off. Use with ladders and boards.

Packing Cases.....

Wooden cases that refrigerators come in are best. They can be sanded, painted and weatherproofed. These cases can be used with ladders, boards, sawhorses, etc.

Large and small cardboard drums.....

Cafeterias receive flour, milk, detergent, etc., in these. cut one or both ends out. Can be used to roll in, as a tunnel, as an accessory for dramatic play, etc.

Large and small wooden boxes.....

Remove any protruding nails or rough areas, sand and paint with different colors. Stack or use side by side. Combine with boards and ladders. Children like to push them, climb inside and sit on top.

Steering wheel box.....

Mount a steering wheel and/or horn into a wooden box or block. A tricycle wheel could also be used.

Pieces of cardboard.....

Uses for these are unlimited! Flat squares can be used to slide down hills. Ropes can be attached to corners and children can pull each other around on grass. Children like to color and paint on cardboard for variety.

Cardboard easel.....

Attach a large square of cardboard to a tree or a fence with string, rope or cord. Use clothespins to hold the paper on the cardboard. The child can hold the paint in a can in his hand or it can be placed on a box next to the easel.

Wooden barrels and kegs.....

Sand and paint each a different color. They can be rolled, climbed inside of or through or used as chairs.

Oil drums.....

Cut out both ends of the oil drums, thoroughly wash and mount on wooden or metal stands.

Concrete sewer pipe.....

Set the pipe into concrete or set it in a slight excavation scooped out in the ground. Another variation is to build steps out of concrete blocks on each side of the pipe so the children can climb up the sides easily.

Tire swing...

Hang an old automobile tire by a rope, 1/2 to 1 inch in diameter, from a tree or from cross bars in an area out of play traffic. Protect the tree limb with tire casing, canvas

or burlap. The tire can be painted a bright color. Punch holes in the bottom to keep water from accumulating. The tire may be hung by one rope like a monkey swing or two ropes like a seat swing.

Tents.....

To make tents, use a pole with canvas, sheets, an old bed-spread, blankets or old drapes. An indoor tent could be made by covering a table with a bedspread.

Tire pump.....

An old tire pump or short lengths of garden hose attached to a block of wood can be used as a gas station or fire engine, etc.

Tire tubes.....

All sizes of inner tubes and automobile tires can be placed around the playground.

Appliances and motors.....

Outside is a good place to allow a child to examine and take apart radios, TVs, automobile and boat motors. Check these for possible danger areas before using with the children.

Car Body.....

An old automobile or jeep body added to the play yard offers unlimited possibilities. Be sure glass windows are taken out, doors are removed and wheels are blocked to prevent moving. A regular size rowboat is fun, too.

Workbench.....

A large packing case (refrigerator) or crate can be used as a workbench for woodworking outside. Boards placed across sawhorses also can make an effective workbench.

Horse.....

Add a pillow or a piece of tire tubing to a sawhorse.

Cardboard boxes.....

There are never enough of these. Use large and small ones. Some could be painted bright colors. Windows and doors could be cut in the larger ones. Moderate and small size cardboard boxes can be stuffed and used for building blocks. Boxes with dividers are particularly useful for this purpose.

Barrel wagon.....

Cut or saw a barrel in half, mount on casters or old skate wheels and attach a rope to the side for pulling.

Sandbox toys.....

Egg cartons, cottage cheese cartons, milk cartons, sifters, sieves, painted cans of all sizes, wooden spoons, measuring spoons, plastic bottles, muffin tins, jello molds, cookie cutters, pans, sugar scoops, coffee pots, ladles, cups, watering cans and wheel toys.

Water play toys.....

Use the following equipment in large tubs or buckets: hoses, pails, corks, shallow pans, kitchen utensils, plastic

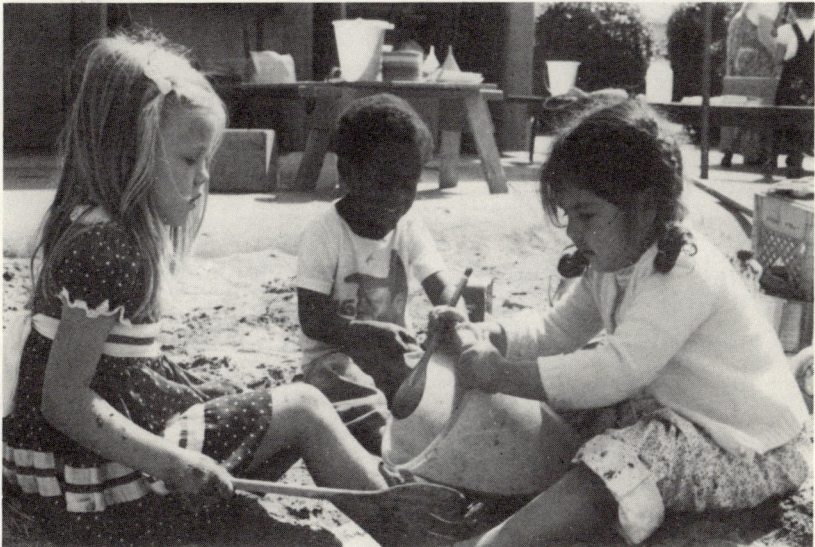

bottles, cups, funnels, sponges, animals cut out of sponges, short lengths of rubber hose, measuring cups, egg beaters, tea kettle, soap, sprinkler tops and dolls.

Poles.....

Saw 2-foot logs from telephone poles. The children can roll over them, stand erect on them, balance on them, jump off of them, etc.

Punch and kick ball.....

Take an old soccer, football or basketball stuffed with excelsior, cotton seeds or sawdust and swing from a tree limb by rope.

Rocks.....

Place *big* rocks around in a circle or unusual formation. Paint them bright colors. Children can jump, sit or walk from one to another.

Log sections.....

Obtain or cut sections different heights. Set in cement on the ground or leave each one movable. Smaller log sections can be used for building.

Sheet target.....

Dye a sheet, cut large and small holes in the sheet. Suspend from a tree limb and throw bean bags or balls at the target.

Box target.....

From a tree limb or bar, suspend a cardboard box 5 feet from the ground. Remove the bottom of the box and on four sides of the box cut out various size holes and throw bean bags or balls through the holes.

Punching bag.....

Hang a stuffed pillow or blue jeans by a rope from a tree limb at children's level.

Sack swing.....

Fill a burlap sack with sawdust. Tie the top of the sack with rope and hang from a tree limb or bars.

Knotted rope.....

Hang from a tree limb or bars a heavy knotted rope, 1 1/4 to 2 inches in diameter. The knots should be 12 to 18 inches apart.

Spring rope.....

From a tree branch 8 to 10 feet from the ground, drop a rope (1 1/2 inches thick) with a heavy coil spring at the top. Tie a knot at the bottom. The bottom should be 14 inches from the ground.

Rings.....

Make a pair of rings out of pieces of rubber hose, tricycle or bicycle tires. Tie to a tree limb or bar with a rope for hanging and/or swinging.

Jumping tube.....

Cover the entire center of an enormous inner tube (3 feet in diameter and 1 foot high when inflated) with canvas for safe bouncing and balancing. Harness the canvas over the tube.

Springs.....

Take an old pair of bed springs (pad a little with old quilts), cover with dark-colored canvas and put in the play yard or in the room on a rainy day.

Mattress.....

Cover an old sanitized mattress with plastic or a washable slip cover. Attach straps so it can be hung on the wall when not in use.

Telephones.....

Make telephones or walkie-talkie sets by tying two cans together some distance apart with string or rope.

Sacks.....

Use clean burlap sacks and dye them different colors. Fill them with sawdust or excelsior and place them around the playground. Also use canvas sacks 18 inches long by 6 inches in diameter and fill with sand. These also make good punching bags.

CREATIVE ACTIVITIES OUTSIDE

Collage.....Use construction paper to paste or glue sticks, leaves, rocks, grass, flowers or anything else gathered from the yard or on a nature walk.

Rocks..... Let the children gather all different sizes of rocks and paint or decorate them using different colored magic markers or tempera paint.

Leaves..... Rake leaves into a large pile for the children to jump, roll or hide in. Let the children rake the leaves, learn about the different shapes or paste them on paper.

Hay..... A bale of hay or straw can be used for children to roll in, load and unload in wagons, rake, etc.

Water
Paint..... Give the children pails, buckets or cans filled with water. Use small paint brushes to paint sidewalks, buildings or toys. Roller brushes give a different effect.

Wash
Clothes.....Let the children wash the doll clothes and hang them on the fence or clothesline.

Mural..... Let several children work together to paint a mural. Place a long piece of shelf paper on the fence with clothespins. Paint can be carried in portable paint tray or soft drink carton with paint cans in the dividers.

Mud Play.. In the summer, section off an area on the dirt playground, add water for mud and play.

Slide..... Use a piece of wax paper to make the slide slick. Let a child slide down the slide sitting on the wax paper.

Bubbles.... Blow clear or colored bubbles outside. Use water, soap, cups or tin juice cans, plastic pipes or paper straws.

Plant a
Garden..... Let the children plant a garden using rakes, trowels, shovels and watering cans. Plant seeds or bulbs that sprout quickly. The children also can look for worms and pill bugs.

Bird
Houses..... Children can make bird feeders out of pans, milk cartons, pine cones, etc.

Finger
paint..... If a table is available outside, finger paint and soap paint can be used on the table top.

Music..... For variety, try a rhythm band outside. Use an extension cord and take the record player.

INDOOR EQUIPMENT

MOVABLE LOCKERS

Each locker can accomodate two children's clothing if hooks are placed on either side. Note that each child has a storage shelf.

Children need some place which belongs only to them, in or near their room. Locker space provides this and the opportunity for children to learn to take responsibility for getting out and putting away their wraps, extra clothes, art products, etc.

Consider the maximum number of children who will be in one room or area. Then study the space where the lockers will be placed. Usually units of two or three are best even though more expensive. This is particularly true for small rooms where space is limited. You may need to place these units separately in various places in the room. Where several groups of children are in one big room, units of four or five or more may be most satisfactory. The use of lockers as dividers is questionable because of the possibility of obstructing the teacher's view for adequate supervision and the relative ease with which they can be tipped over, unless special provision is made for stability. For larger children, increase the height of the lower section to 33" - 36". This necessarily increases the total height proportionately.

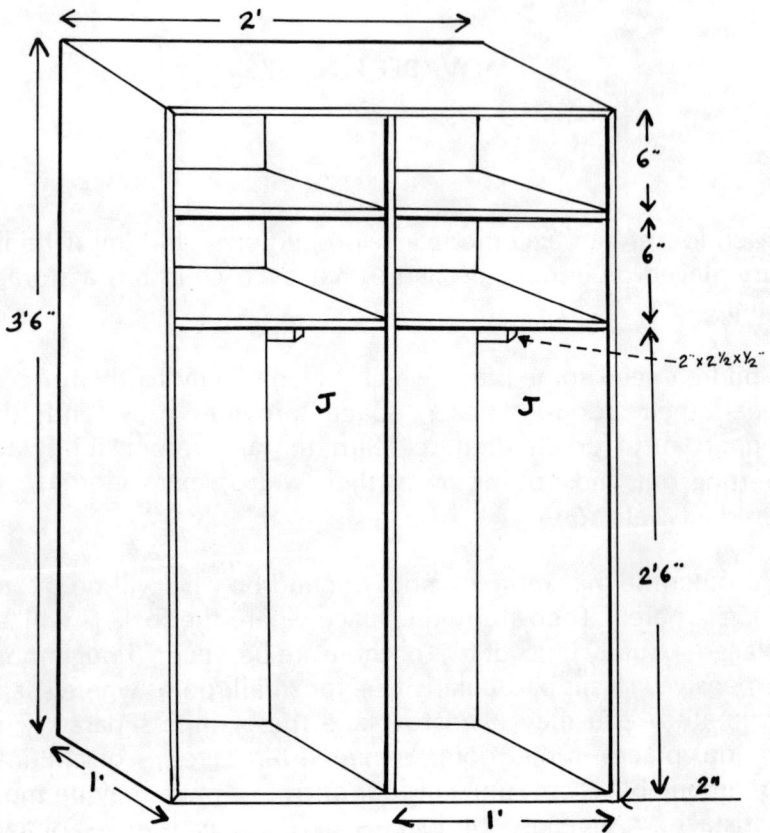

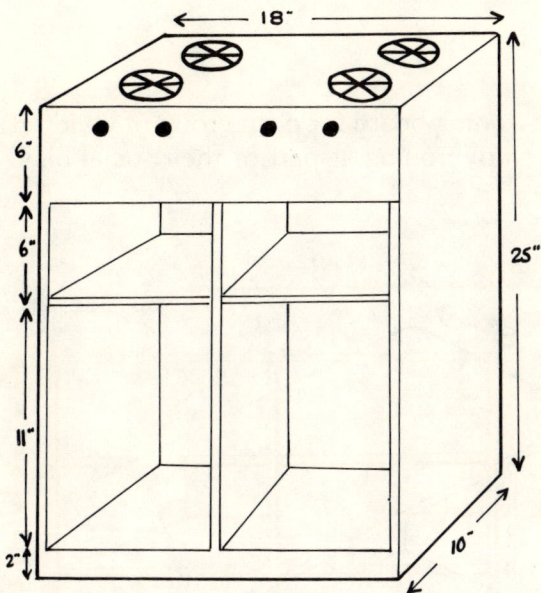

STOVE FOR HOUSEKEEPING CENTER

The stove and the table are the two most basic pieces of house-keeping area equipment.

Paint on the burner markings. The four knobs should turn. Make the knobs from half-spools, wooden beads or purchased knobs.

This stove provides two shelves for storage of play dishes, pans, groceries, etc. Adding doors to the lower section is not necessary, but would provide another interesting experience for the children.

IRONING BOARD FOR HOUSEKEEPING AREA

Provide one ironing board for each group of children. Children thoroughly enjoy ironing as part of their social play.

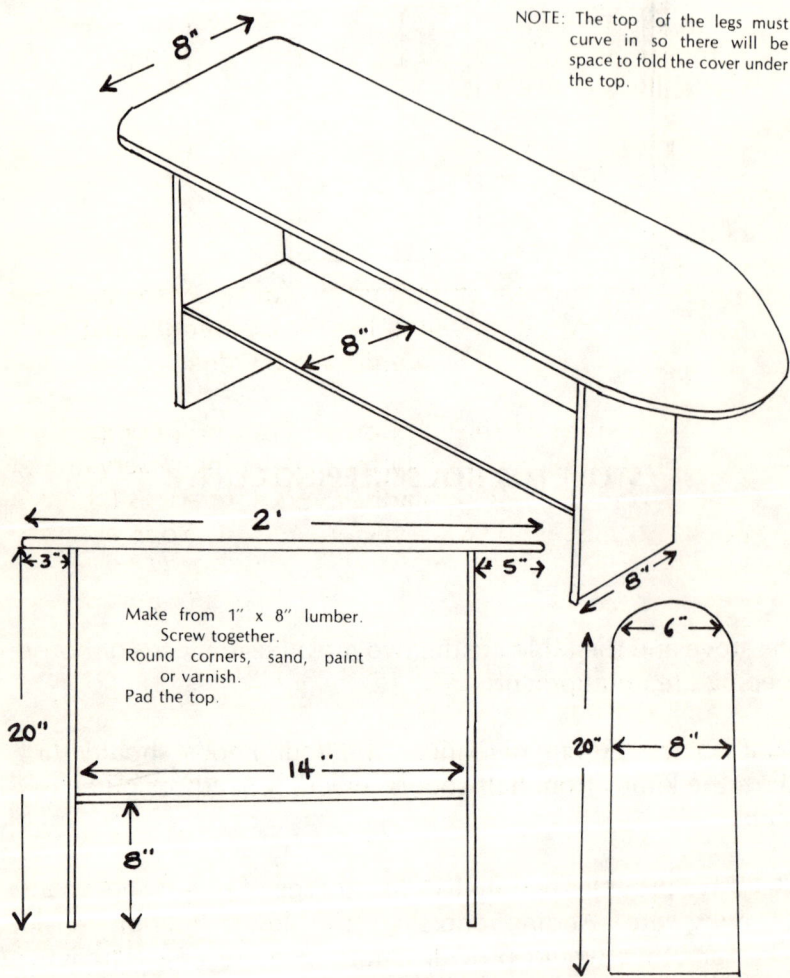

NOTE: The top of the legs must curve in so there will be space to fold the cover under the top.

8"

8"

8"

2'

3"

5"

8"

Make from 1" x 8" lumber.
Screw together.
Round corners, sand, paint
or varnish.
Pad the top.

20"

14"

8"

6"

20"

8"

MIRRORS IN THE CLASSROOM

The most important mirror for the classroom should be:

Full length - as tall as the tallest child

Positioned so the child can see himself from his feet to his head when he is close.

Movable (on a stand) so it can be used for different purposes, in different places and both horizontally and vertically.

Purposes

For the development of positive self-image. Many children have no idea what they look like. It is essential that each child identify himself as a unique individual.

For comparison of self with others, not in a competitive sense, but as an opportunity for developing observational skills and identifying similarities and differences ("I am a boy. You are a girl. My eyes are brown. Your eyes are blue.")

For use as a teaching tool.
Identification: Names of parts - mirror, stand, etc.
Relationship: Front, back, top, bottom, etc.
Characteristics: Fragility of mirror and stand; understanding of how it is to be used and cared for.

Young children who are not interested in grooming or health care, except as play as they wash, etc., can be encouraged to look in the mirror to see if they have removed their chocolate pudding. Older children can actually check to see if their hair is combed, buttons fastened, etc., and use the mirror as a grooming aid.

The mirror can nurture creative dramatics. How interesting it is to observe ones own body movements, facial expressions, appearance in improvised costumes.

Units involving such things as playing shoe store or buying clothes will be enriched with the mirror.

Informal practice in identifying parts of the body, body movements, clothing, occurs logically in front of the mirror. (Do not teach left and right in front of the mirror.)

Talking about different types and uses of mirrors is interesting: the dentist mirror, the car rear-view mirror, signaling with mirrors, and others.

CONSTRUCTION OF FLANNELBOARDS

For construction of triangular, self-standing flannelboard, select a corrugated cardboard box of the size needed for the flannelboard. Remove one side and ends. If the sides are not equal widths, remove the narrow side. Tape remaining three sides together forming a triangular shap. Two sides or all three sides may be covered with flannel or felt, which should be stretched smoothly over the outer surface, folded under to the inside of box and secured with staples or masking tape.

For a folding flannelboard, two pieces of plywood may be hinged and the front covered with flannel. Two sides of a large cardboard box may be hinged with tape and covered with flannel. Stretch flannel smoothly over the front surface, fold to the back and secure with staples or masking tape. Handles may be attached for easy carrying.

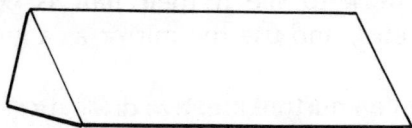

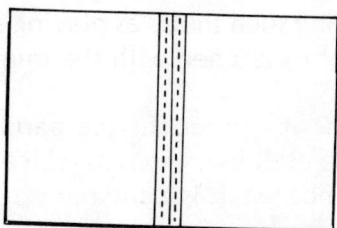

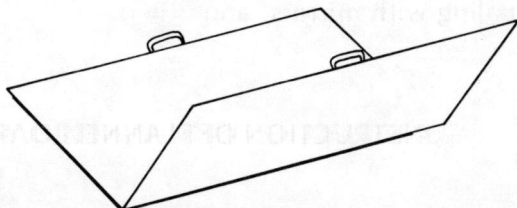

Individual boards may be constructed from shirt cardboard or cardboard from boxes (12″ x 18″) and covered with flannel or felt. Stretch the flannel smoothly over the front surface and glue or tape to the back. These may be used so that each child would have one on which to manipulate accessories.

---

* See pamphlet on *"Creative Teaching Through Bulletin Boards"* for further information and usage of flannelboards and bulletin boards.